SMALL TALK

*The Definitive Guide to Talking to Anyone in Any Situation
(The Art of Having Small Conversations That Lead to Big
Things)*

Kenneth Moreno

Published By Zoe Lawson

Kenneth Moreno

All Rights Reserved

Small Talk: The Definitive Guide to Talking to Anyone in Any Situation (The Art of Having Small Conversations That Lead to Big Things)

ISBN 978-1-77485-305-4

All rights reserved. No part of this guide may be reproduced in any form without permission in writing from the publisher except in the case of brief quotations embodied in critical articles or reviews.

Legal & Disclaimer

The information contained in this book is not designed to replace or take the place of any form of medicine or professional medical advice. The information in this book has been provided for educational and entertainment purposes only.

The information contained in this book has been compiled from sources deemed reliable, and it is accurate to the best of the Author's knowledge; however, the Author cannot guarantee its accuracy and validity and cannot be held liable for any errors or omissions. Changes are periodically made to this book. You must consult your doctor or get professional medical advice before using any of the suggested remedies, techniques, or information in this book.

Upon using the information contained in this book, you agree to hold harmless the Author from and against any damages, costs, and expenses, including any legal fees potentially resulting from the application of any of the information provided by this guide. This disclaimer applies to any damages or injury caused by the use and application, whether directly or indirectly, of any advice or information presented, whether for breach of contract, tort, negligence, personal injury, criminal intent, or under any other cause of action.

You agree to accept all risks of using the information presented inside this book. You need to consult a professional medical practitioner in order to ensure you are both able and healthy enough to participate in this program.

TABLE OF CONTENTS

INTRODUCTION 1

CHAPTER 1: WHAT TO DECIDE TO GO OUT INSTEAD OF STAYING HOME 3

CHAPTER 2: RESOLVING SOCIAL ANXIETY 13

CHAPTER 3: SOCIAL SKILLS AND HOW TO DEVELOP GOOD SOCIAL SKILLS 21

CHAPTER 4: FIVE MOST IMPORTANT QUESTIONS YOU MUST TO ANSWER 28

CHAPTER 5: THE BODY LANGUAGE OF YOUR BODY SAYS EVERYTHING 36

CHAPTER 6: WHAT YOU CAN DO TO ENHANCE YOUR SOCIAL SKILLS 41

CHAPTER 7: A GOOD CONVERSATION GUIDES: THINGS TO DISCUSS 62

CHAPTER 8: LEARNING THE ART OF SMALL TALK 74

CHAPTER 9: CREATIVE STRATEGIES TO BEGIN SMALL TALKS 87

CHAPTER 10: LISTENING, AND KNOWLEDGE 97

CHAPTER 11: CONVERSATIONS WITH OTHERS 117

CHAPTER 12: WHAT TO BEGIN WITH SMALL TALK 136

CHAPTER 13: THE BEST WAY TO BEGIN A CONVERSATION 144

CHAPTER 14: PRESENTING BODY LANGUAGE THAT IS APPROACHABLE 152

CHAPTER 15: DISPLAY YOUR PERSONALITY 157

CHAPTER 16: UTILIZING CONVERSATION TO MAKE DEEP CONNECTIONS 163

CHAPTER 17: AVOID UNFORTUNATE SILENCES 170

CONCLUSION 180

Introduction

Some people are so sexy they are so adept at making small talk, and then fail on their first attempt. Small talk is a great thing. It can bring you many new acquaintances, and even possibly a potential spouse! You never know! For those who are shy and feel out of place every time they encounter a stranger small talk isn't always an alternative.

It is not necessary to be a person of the crowd However, there is a lot you can master the art of communication. From breaking the ice, to how you can end the palaver, it shouldn't be too difficult for you thanks to the advice we will provide to you within this Book.

One of the most crucial pieces advice is to .... Get started! You'll stumble in the beginning before you'll become proficient at it. It is true that making conversationand maintaining it for a long time with strangers requires some practice.

Set yourself a goal such as, say, making small talks with two strangers per day! This is among the most effective methods of expanding your circle of friends. Always seek out occasions to make friends, and you'll be surprised you'll find a lot of people seeking new acquaintances.

It's normal to be uncomfortable for the first few occasions. With time you'll be as elegant and elegant as Will Smith.

Chapter 1: What to Decide To Go Out Instead of staying home

To enhance my life my introvert side has been a victim in my life because I am constantly challenging it. As a child of the baby, I discovered it difficult to sit in my home and relax, but as an introverted, I would always shiver at the thought of leaving. This led to two forces of my life constantly clashed in my own world. This led me to learn how to find balance and harmony between these two forces.

After completing my Bachelor's program I went to Europe for my Master's. Although I was thrilled by the idea of leaving my home country but it was a difficult decision to take. This wasn't only because it was totally outside the comfort zones of me, but it also meant that I needed to meet new friends, make new friends, and, in essence, rebuild my life as a social person.

When I arrived in that place, I became extremely nervous as I had no person there.

Because of my introverted nature, I was immediately drawn to the idea of living on my own in this new place, while I concentrated on my research. But, on the same note the idea of meeting new people and forming new connections socializing, having a drink, socializing and being nice in a foreign land was a bit daunting for me.

To soothe my lonely self in this city of fear I chose to think about the wise words my mother used to tell me "You are always welcome home" she told me. The words of that mother were never distant from my thoughts, as I found them soothing when I was in the worst of moments.

The home is always warm as well as warm and secure. The idea of returning home on the whim of a moment was a constant source of motivation, confidence and relaxed. Thus, this thought became an energy source for me when I was in introverted circumstances.

My mom used to make the comment I was hesitant to accept it as it didn't make sense to me. When she asked me about it, I replied, "Mum I am going to be 2,500 miles away, which is roughly 1,553 miles. How do you define by you can always return to home?"

She said, "Of course you can. If you enjoy the company of people in your new town You will find your own home there. You can also return back home. If you don't like the crowd living in the city, you are able to leave and return home".

This powerful phrase stayed for me as I was getting on my plane to start my journey towards this land. When we were in air, I would repeatedly repeat to myself "All is going to be fine since you'll always be able to return to home... You'll succeed". I could probably repeat this phrase to myself about 10 times before I experienced the calmness around me, and my worry about the new city slowed down.

It's the same to going out and you don't like the atmosphere there then guess what? You are able to go back home.

Human nature is innate and can provide a thousand excuses as to that you shouldn't stay at home.

"The location for the party is too far away. Instead of spending all that time driving I'd rather spend it on something else productive".

"That event is taking place on the other side of town. The tickets for transport cost each $10 to get there, which is very expensive".

"My friends wouldn't be attending the event. If they had been there I would have been there too".

In all the excuses mentioned above, there is a common thread appears to be that you'll always find a reason not go. Instead, try to persuade your thoughts to discover reasons to go. If for any reason, you aren't enjoying the experience as much, are aware that you can always return home.

The act of trying an event doesn't mean you have to remain there for the rest of your life.

Answering "yes" to a friend's message to hang out does not mean you have to spend three hours or an entire night there.

This means that you're willing to make the event or gathering a portion of your time, but you are able to go home whenever you want to.

Remember that what trying really means is that you'll be there. There is nothing more.

If an invitation to an event explicitly demand a commitment of an amount of time it is possible to stay clear of making commitments like this by simply saying, "Let's see how it is".

If you are getting an invitation to attend an event in particular Let me walk you through the process of thinking:

You get a text message "Hey Do you wish for a night out?"

It is obvious that you don't know the specifics of the occasion or celebration. It is a matter of whether it is a good thing or not. In the present you're uncertain about whether or not you'd like to attend this event. In response to this uncertainty you are hesitant to attend. In some instances the reason for this is because your instinctual, the habit that you've developed over time, prevails in the most common reaction to these situations and that is to refuse to go.

For an introvert who wants to be social The reality is that you are able to walk by the event to assess the scene and determine whether or not like to attend. If you don't then guess what? You are always able to go home.

To better comprehend the specifics of each situation it is important to understand how to distinguish between the motives behind your decision to not take part in. Are you letting your flight instinct kick into action because you feel easier to stay at home ? Or are you opting to stay at home as it's the most rational option based on your thorough assessment of the situation.

Like in every situation there are always choices to make for instance, would you rather do your work or attend a gathering; refresh your energy or attend a host a party? Prepare an official presentation or just hang out.

The point I'm trying to get across is that it's okay to remain at home if there is a legitimate reason to do it. To avoid situations of 'one size is all you need', act prudently when you have to be at home to do something, or recharge your energy. However If you don't take advantage of every opportunity to get out, don't forget the first rule: you'll always be able to return home.

This method works perfectly with calls , too.

One specific day I experienced an extremely hectic working day. I had a lot of conversations and had to travel the extra mile, and when I finally got back home I felt exhausted. One of the things I didn't want was to talk to anyone. My boyfriend at the time informed him "Let's make a phone call. I'm required to talk to you about something". My first thought was Do not tell me today. Don't do it now. I was so scared, but I needed to take control of my mind by telling myself "You can always stop any conversation". As a general rule I do to keep in mind that no one is able to make me maintain a conversation for more than one hour. I prefer five minutes of conversation with someone with whom we both provide as much value as we can rather than engaging in an hour-long conversation regarding spilled milk. If I feel that I'm not able to engage in any conversation, or that I don't have anything of benefit to give to the listener I will usually declare, "As much as I enjoyed talking to you, I'm really forced to go".

Chapter 2: Resolving Social Anxiety

Social anxiety can be a very frustrating mental disorder which can be addressed in a variety of simple and effective methods. It is a disorder that can control your life and keep your from socializing with people around you. There are many effective methods to help you overcome social anxiety. Some of them are described in the following paragraphs:

Positive Thinking

If you are looking to conquer social anxiety, it's essential that you use positive thoughts and emotions. Positive thinking is among the most effective methods to make you feel comfortable and overcome any challenges. Begin by imagining the importance, value and valuable you are. This will achieve a sense of peace that allows your mind and body to ease.

Positive feelings and thoughts are beneficial because they can be very satisfying and satisfying. They can assist you in achieving a sense of achievement. If you don't believe in yourself or think of yourself as an important individual, you're more likely suffer from social anxiety. We all have the same qualities but if you do not feel that you're valuable, then you'll start to be afraid of others and begin to isolate yourself. This can reduce your happiness and hinder you from living an enjoyable and satisfying life. Therefore, it is important to focus on positive thoughts to feel content with your own self and make friends.

Visualization

Visualization is the process of creating mental or mental images of the ideal you want to portray. If you are looking to overcome with social anxiety , think about imagining yourself in social settings and then respond to the situation in the manner you would have if that it had actually happened. Through imagining yourself in a crowd and speaking confidently and with confidence, you will learn how to build efficient social abilities. Visualization is a method of learning which helps you change your thinking. It helps you communicate and talk confidently in any social setting. The more you can visualize, the more likely you will be to overcome your social anxiety and begin to talk to people in the real world.

Mindfulness

The first step in overcoming beat social anxiety is to practice mindfulness, as it helps to be present moment with your experience. Living in the present can help you in getting rid of your anxiety and worries and get started living a joyful and healthy life. Mindfulness is the best way to be aware of your thoughts and feelings as well as your emotions without making any judgements or thinking over the near or the past. It can bring a sense of peace and relaxation that are vital when it comes to getting rid of social anxiety.

Self-Love

Self-love is one of the most important aspects in conquering social anxiety as it's all about loving admiring, appreciating, and feeling good about yourself. This is a crucial step to take if you wish to improve your overall health and well-being. It is important to be aware of the strengths as well as weaknesses, and ensure that you don't let anything undermine your self-esteem. If you're in love with yourself, you won't feel the need to gain the approval or respect of others. Self-love is a way to manage social anxiety since it gives you the confidence and self-esteem. Self-love can help you get rid of any negative thoughts or feelings you may be experiencing. If you're self-loved other people will also be taught to love you , and this will make you feel more secure and comfortable.

Meet People

Meeting new people and making acquaintances is a great method of improving your social skills as well as combating social anxiety. It's not easy to meet new people but after a while, you'll become comfortable with it and understand what's wrong and how you'll manage it. Interacting with different types of people can also allow you connect with people who love and respect your self-worth. This makes you feel good about yourself and will encourage you to continue having fun. There are people you meet who don't judge, but understand what you're experiencing and are likely to try to cheer you up and make sure you feel loved and valued. Get out and meet other people who bring out the best out of your personality and help you overcome your anxieties and fears.

Surmont Your Fears

There is always a bit of anxiety throughout our lives, but you must be able to confront these fears confidently and stand out as an individual. Fear often stifles us and causes us to live miserable lives. If you want to achieve satisfaction and happiness in your daily life then you must learn to conquer your fears and anxieties. Self-confidence can help you overcome your fears and assist you relax and learn how to manage things differently. Believing in yourself and speaking with others without being critical of yourself will allow you to overcome your anxieties and increase your social abilities. If you are afraid to talk with your friends, it is recommended to practice speaking to one friends, and then move on to two, and then further. This will boost confidence in yourself and make you feel more confident and comfortable with your friends.

Make Healthy Habits

Our lifestyles are crucial and if we are looking to get rid of social anxiety, we should make the necessary adjustments to our habits. Healthy routines include eating healthy food exercise, getting fit, eliminating stress, and getting enough sleep , etc. It could be your are or what you do that make you feel uncomfortable talking the time to talk to others. It is therefore important to look after yourself and begin to practice healthy habits that enable you to love and respect yourself.

Don't allow your appearance or behaviour influence how you choose to interact with others, however, you can develop ways to increase your confidence.

Chapter 3: Social Skills and How to Develop Good Social Skills

Social skills are essential in overcoming social anxiety and shyness. These abilities are crucial to maintain and build relationships with others They are typically described as the capacity to alter one's behavior accordance with a certain circumstance. This is the way that we interact and communicate whether it's through verbal or non-verbal methods and how we express our thoughts and emotions to others.

Many may believe that the exuberant and extrovert manner of interaction with others is the appropriate type of social ability but it's not the most effective and sole method of effectively communicating with other people. Even those with shyness or introversion could build a solid set of interpersonal skills that enable them to build and sustain successful interpersonal relationships that have long-lasting effects on one's life.

Social skills are learned early throughout a person's lifetime. When they are children, human beings frequently interact with each other through imitation of the models presented to them. The majority of the time, the way parents and relatives behave is the ways that children behave in their daily lives. For instance parents who are courteous tend towards having children who are also likely to be considerate.

However those who live with adults who regularly curse are likely to develop the behavior and eventually learn to curse too. It is important to keep in mind because most parents will leave teaching to daycare or education system, yet the fact of the issue is that they will always be the primary teachers their children be taught by. This being said, if you would like your child to improve their social skills it is important to instruct them by the example of others.

Children develop social skills on their own But there are those who require proper guidance to ensure they do not have to be battling to form relationships. It shouldn't be a surprise to learn that how children interact isn't what parents expect from their children. Of course, the ideal scenario is for children to come to know one another and to play with each other and build friendships However, there are instances of bullying, teasing or children being insecure enough to not interact with other children.

One of the most effective ways to help children develop excellent social skills is to be exposed to positive interactions. This is the reason why children who live with other children usually have a better chance of developing friendships with other children. Children who don't experience the same social environment as children older than them will require help from those with more experience. If you would like your child to improve their social skills it is essential to talk to them and help them become at ease with human interactions. Begin by having conversations as simple as asking your child how their day was or if they have gained any new knowledge at school.

It is also beneficial to talk to your child about the things you like. At an early age, children will be able to communicate effectively with other people, and by bringing out their passions, they will gain confidence and feel positive on themselves. It is important that parents do the right things with their children and provide them with positive reinforcements.

Of of course, not all children are able to develop great social abilities. People who are found to be anxious or shy in social settings have a harder time learning to be a good social person however, it doesn't mean they'll have to deal with anxiety throughout their life. Particularly in the case of adolescents, human beings naturally develop and realize how social relationships are an essential aspect of life. This is the reason why anxieties and shyness must be dealt with as quickly as is possible.

For children, the most effective way to improve social skills of all human beings regardless of age is to engaging in conversation with others. This is a bit more difficult than it sounds People should engage in human interactions to improve their social skills and also their relationships. Participate in conversations, whether with people you feel familiar with or with total strangers.

If you are unsure about speaking up, attempt to practice what you do in your head. Make a list of conversation starters even when you're alone and consider what you can do to best respond to specific circumstances. If, for instance, someone asks you to meet up then think of how you can best respond. Instead of just thinking about what you would say, you must try to speak the words to ensure you're more certain that you'll be able to do it in real life in the future.

Self-esteem is very crucial for developing good social skills. Build this confidence by learning more about yourself and learning what you excel at. The most effective way to boost self-confidence is to get out and demonstrate to others the qualities you possess. In the end, there's nothing more powerful for self-esteem than receiving positive praise from other people.

Chapter 4: Five most important questions You Must to Answer

Now (with your recording device on) respond to these five commonly asked small talk questions like you were speaking with Bob or Jessica (or the person you invented).

Your name is what?

Where do you come where are you?

What are you doing?

Who is it that you are here with?

What can you do to have amusement?

After you've responded and recorded all questions, replay it and are feeling about the way it is sounding. Be attentive at your own voice. What did it sound like? If you could draw an image of your voice, how do you think it would appear like? Did you talk too fast (or slow)? Remember these questions for the next part of the course since you'll discover how to adjust the sound of your voice exactly the way you would like you to.

Perform this exercise a second time and apply these techniques to your responses.

Where do you come where are you?

Make sure you include something unique or interesting about your city in response to this question. For instance, don't simply mention, "I'm from Fresno." You can say, "I'm from Fresno, the city in which raisins were invented and also one of the biggest blues festivals across the country."

This creates an interesting topic to discuss and your listener is much more likely to recall who you are connecting you to those distinctive facts.

What can you do?

If you are a person who gives brief one or two-word answers, it's the right the right time to alter your approach now. For instance, if you're a computer programmer rather than saying "I'm computer programmer" then you could use something that the majority of people will be able to relate to, for example "I develop computer programs to help children to learn a new the language" (or whatever subject you are working with). It is important to make it clear who you're helping and the way you help them.

If you do this, you'll be communicating in the same way so that people can comprehend the things you're spending the majority of your time doing. If you were to say, "I'm a computer programmer," the response you'd get will most likely be negative because the majority of people aren't aware of what a computer programmer does or does, not simply because their heads are way up above the clouds to admit the fact that it is.

Therefore, take just a few minutes to come up with an entirely new phrase or two of what you've done.

Who do you help?

How can you help them?

Who are you with? How do you get to know each other?

If you're with someone, you can simply introduce yourself and provide an interesting fact about them. For instance, "This is Jerry. He's traveled the world , and just came back from Africa this week." Or "This is Sally. She is a teacher for students with disabilities and has won her teacher of the month award twice months in two months."

It's crucial to state something that is unique to the person you're talking to since it makes the person you are with look nice (and they'll be grateful for it) and makes you sound like someone who is humble and people are drawn to. If you're not sure about the person you're with, don't worry - ask them to share something special about them.

What can you do to have enjoyment?

Find the things you love doing during your spare time. If it's playing golf, watching the latest film as well as meeting up with new friends at coffee shops, you need to make your story interesting enough that others can appreciate the things you enjoy doing for pleasure. When answering this question it is important to think about "Why am I enjoying engaging in this activity?"

For instance what is the reason you go to golf? Instead of telling people "golf" you could offer a reason to help your listener know why you play golf. For instance, you could say "I enjoy kicking the golf ball with a group of acquaintances. It's a great way to exercise and to be outdoors and I'm going to play for the tournament in my local area in July."

If you add these five small-talking tricks to your bag of conversational skills, you'll outdo the vast majority of the people who are out there.

After you've incorporated the new methods, you can go on and take notes of your answers to the questions you asked. Listen to it and check what you sound like.

The Tone

A person's voice can be the difference between success or failure in the very first couple of seconds in your conversation. So it is crucial to make sure your voice is in the right place you would like it to be in order to show enthusiasm, passion and confidence in your self as we will discuss in the in the next section.

Note down what you enjoy and dislike. Take note of your voice and how it is sounded. If you have something you'd like to improve regarding it, then it's time to take action.

You might have a strong voice or you are feeling your voice is high or low, or maybe you have a lisp which you do not like. Maybe you're a visual individual and you're not in a position to convey every thing you see. In this the case you talk too quickly and it's difficult for people to comprehend your voice. All of these assumptions will affect your confidence in your abilities to communicate, and influence how people react to you.

Chapter 5: The Body Language of Your Body Says Everything

Your body language can be an important component in establishing small conversation. The way you conduct yourself when talking to a stranger, and between conversations can affect the pace of conversation.

The right body language skills is vital to keep conversations going. It encourages your partner to take part and enhances the impression they have of the person you are talking to. It is therefore crucial to keep your attitude throughout the discussion. Otherwise, you could be lost to the other person.

It is not common for everyone to have the proper body language. But, it is possible to learn how to conduct yourself when speaking. You can learn this by watching the movies of famous musicians, actors or even national leaders.

Examine how they stand and talk, then mimic what they do. When you first meet someone it may seem like you're faking but over time it will be part of your. This will be helpful when you wish to meet new people.

First, make sure to make sure your arms and legs remain open. People love to fold their hands inwards and lay their arms across their bodies. If you're looking to have a successful conversation ensure that your hands are open when conversing with the other person.

Legs and arms crossed will make you appear protective or cautious. People are not a fan of working with people who are defensive.

Another vital body language component that you should use when engaging when talking to others includes eye contact. It is important to keep an eye-to-eye contact with anyone you're speaking to. This lets them know that you're attentive and appreciate the topic you're talking about.

While it's nice to look at the stranger, don't overdo it. It is rude to stare and can cause someone to be scared away. However If you don't maintain eye contact, you'll look unsecure.

When you're having a conversation, it's essential to appear confident. Even if you're supposed to maintain a distance, stand and sit with your legs in a straight line. The tension can increase when you're speaking to an unfamiliar person. Take your shoulders off to ease off tension.

The only way to ensure that the person is in conversation mode is when they know you value the person. Make sure to smile every time you are speaking and to show your support for the words they are using. If you're sitting in a place, you should not slump across the seat; instead, sit straight.

Lean a little towards the person However, not too excessively. While doing this smile and smile and laugh. This will make the conversation and help the other person to keep talking. Be positive all the time since people are drawn to those who have positive outlooks. Be sure to keep your fingers away off your face. It could lead to distraction during the conversation. It is in conjunction with keeping your head elevated. The fact that you are looking at the ground continuously can make you appear unsecure.

Finally, instead of fiddling using your legs and fingers instead, use them to talk about problems. This will allow you to let the other person comprehend what you're telling them. In the end, body language is essential to a successful small talk.

Chapter 6: What You Can Do to Enhance Your Social Skills

Human beings are unique from other animals is their capacity to communicate using languages and build relationships. Through communication, humans interact in order to satisfy diverse demands. The thing that allows humans to communicate and interact with other people is their social skills. This article is designed to give useful tips to help you improve your social skills, including how to establish goals as well as the importance of having empathy, and the best way to connect with people and become acquaintances. The article also provides valuable tips on how you can comprehend yourself and others well.

The Definition and Importance of Social Skills

Social skills are the abilities that allow humans to interact, communicate and establish peaceful interpersonal relationships. Social interaction includes a myriad of components that include the capacity to interact, influence and establish harmonious relationships. There are several types of communication. This includes groups of communication, interpersonal communication, social media as well as communication via mainstream media. Communication is also classified as verbal, written, and non-verbal. Writing communication is the process of using written symbols to communicate while verbal communication is the act of transmitting a message using spoken words. If you speak verbally, you're expected to utilize various nonverbal signals of communication. These are gestures, cues and facial expressions are used when you speak.

Social skills are crucial for any form of communication. These skills allow you to communicate with others effectively. Additionally, if you have social skills, people are more likely to be attentive to your message. There are many benefits to having social abilities. This includes:

The creation of a welcoming workplace - Employees who are socially adept are able to communicate well with other people and reduce the likelihood of conflict. Leaders who have social abilities are able to comprehend others and employ methods of influence to make them feel more comfortable.

Knowledge acquisition - If you're a socially adept person are able to communicate with people of different backgrounds and acquire a wealth of information. The knowledge you gain helps you reduce conflicts.

Expanding your network If you're a social person you'll be able to connect with a variety of people from different backgrounds. A few of them could have opportunities that can aid you in improving your financial situation.

Sharing your views - When you have excellent social skills are able to offer your personal perspectives on various issues. Your perspectives can help others.

In a state of focus - with social skills, you'll be in a position to be focused in achieving common goals.

Growth of your business If you're a person with impressive social skills, others will be positive about you, which can attract others to your offerings. With these referrals they will allow you to expand your business, with only a tiny amount of marketing.

Qualities That Improve Social Skills

Social skills are crucial for anyone who wishes to succeed in life. These skills assist us in creating and sustain relationships. If you're looking to develop your social skills, there is various qualities you need to develop. These include:

Effective communication is a crucial component of social abilities. Communication can assist you in expressing your thoughts in a way that is effective and brings them to the top of your list. If you're a good communicator and collaboration, you can put an entire team together with the aim of reaching goals.

Conflict resolution is a key component of any social situation conflict can arise. As a person of authority who has outstanding social skills, you'll be competent to handle these conflicts peacefully.

Active listening - Listening actively means paying the attention of what is being said. If you are attentive to another person you will be able to show them respect for them and appreciate you. There are a variety of strategies you can apply to be uninhibited listeners. This includes Avoiding distractions, paying attention to the content of what's being said, and making sure you are prepared to respond and ask questions.

Empathy allows you to place yourself in the shoes of other people and feel their feelings. A person who is empathetic takes note of the emotions of others. Through the development of empathy skills that allow you to build strong bonds with people.

Relationship Management Social skills are crucial for managing relationships. If you manage relationships, it implies that you're able connect with clients in a specific way and build solid bonds with them.

Respect is an important aspect of communication. If you're respectful of your fellows and are capable of letting them speak things with no interruption. Also, you appreciate others in their communication by asking relevant and thoughtful questions, staying focused on the subject and avoiding unnecessary time.

Strategies for Enhancing Your Social Skills

Asking for feedback To improve your social abilities by asking your most trusted friends and coworkers to provide you with feedback of areas they believe you could improve on. It is important to choose honest feedback that you can use to develop your social abilities.

Create Goals - If you identify areas for improvement, it's important to develop a strategy on how you can be better. When you make your proposal, be sure that you've established specific goals that are measurable and precise.

Find resources - There are many resources to assist you to improve your social abilities. This can be done through online sites, studying pertinent books, and attending certain classes.

Practice - Once you've learned the different strategies to improve your social abilities, it's vital that you put the knowledge you've learned into action. It is possible to begin exercising at the workplace or at home.

Continue to Learn - The best way to improve your social abilities is to keep on learning.

What is the best way to set goals?

Each aspect of our work needs a plan. This is accomplished by having clear objectives. They are the specific goals you'd like to achieve whenever you do something. If you're hoping to succeed in the process of setting goals you must follow a series of steps you must adhere to. This article offers suggestions on how to set goals within whatever plans you've got.

Note them down. There is nothing you can call the goal if you've not written it down. The idea that you have in your head isn't a target until it is written down. The purpose of writing your goals down in order to make their meaning and help them to be remembered. It is easy to lose goals that reside in your mind.

Be precise regarding Goals Beyond noting them down It is vital to make sure that the goals are precise. If goals are precise they are quantifiable, and progress can be measured. Specific goals are specific and written in simple language.

A specific timeframe is essential to specify the time frame you'll need to meet your goals. When you list the date, month and year for attaining your goal, you'll be more focused on getting it. It is essential to utilize an organized calendar and establish an accurate timeframe within which the goal can be achieved.

What is the reason you're trying to reach the objective - It's important to understand the motives behind this goal. In addition, to explain why you're determined to achieve it the goal. You must provide an argument that is compelling as to what you want to achieve. For example, the purpose of exercising is to shed weight and increase your fitness. If you have a motive for setting your goal, you become committed to achieving it.

Goals must be quantifiable - When you formulate goals, it's crucial to make sure they're quantifiable so that you can keep track of your progress toward reaching the goals. It should be a particular measure that aids in tracking performance of goals. For example, if are looking to shed 50kgs of weight in five months, then you need to try to reduce your weight to 10kgs per month. When you have goals that you can measure it becomes much easier to monitor their growth and progress toward achieving these goals.

Massive Action Plan (MAP) A massive action program is a specific plan for how you will achieve your objectives. It includes strategies methods, strategies, and methods to follow in reaching your goal. That is your MAP should address the "how" question. For instance, if you're looking to lose 50kg of your weight within five months, you must identify the strategies and methods you'll use. This could include exercising at the gym, and also dieting.

Recognize your limiting beliefs You may have a variety of beliefs you might be able to block your strategy for achieving your goals. It is important to recognize these beliefs and then work to overcome them. For example, you're a single woman searching for a trustworthy male companion for marriage. Your belief is that all men lie. This negative belief could hinder your strategy for achieving your goals and must be eliminated. It is important to write down the beliefs that limit you and then come up with the best strategy to get rid of these beliefs.

Mental objections - In addition to the beliefs that limit you There are also spiritual issues that you should be prepared to face. Psychological complaints are ideas that we've created in our minds through listening to what our friends tell us. For example, a friend might suggest to them that losing weight can be delicate, and it will take much of your time. If you're trying to lose weight, it is important to get rid of this idea to ensure that it doesn't hinder your progress.

Time management - It's impossible to reach your goals if you aren't managing your time efficiently. It's crucial to schedule time to work towards your goals. During that time, be sure that you do not engage in time wasters as well as any other distractions. It is possible to use time management tools available via the internet.

The process of tracking your performance is important. You must have an effective method of measuring your progress towards goal accomplishment. For instance, you could break down your goals into smaller chunks to allow you to easily monitor your progress on an ongoing or weekly basis. For example, if your objective was to shed 50kg by the end of five months, it is essential to be able to track whether you're losing 10 kgs on the monthly basis.

How to Increase Your Empathy

Empathy is the capacity to understand the feelings of others. A person who is compassionate is adept at understanding someone else's concerns and suggest solutions. There are many aspects of empathy you have to master. This includes:

Listening skills - An empathetic person has good listening skills. If you're a person with an excellent level of listening is when you don't interrupt other people when they're speaking, and you ask pertinent questions and offer thoughtful remarks. It's important to be kind and understanding since people will be more likely to trust you.

Attention - Being attentive means that you are more focused on what someone else is talking about. It is best to stay clear of distractions that could cause you to not be able to hear to the conversation. It is also important to not interrupt your partner while they're talking.

Learn to appreciate the cultures of other people Empathic skills are developed by learning to appreciate different cultures. This means that you often travel to meet people from different backgrounds. If you can understand the motives that people behave in the way it is, you'll become compassionate and begin to understand their behavior without bias.

Feedback Request It is recommended that your friends to offer suggestions for how to improve your listening abilities. After receiving feedback, you need to come up with an approach to implement the suggestions. It's best if you were also able to work in various areas that you're working on.

The reading genre includes many books that deal with the subject of empathy. It's important to find these books and then read them to develop your ability to empathize. There are also useful resources on the internet to shed some more light on the topic of empathy.

Assess your biases. To become empathetic it is essential to look at our biases regarding others that prevent us from listening with empathy. Perhaps you are biased towards someone due to their race, colour or gender. If you can eliminate these biases, you'll develop your empathy skills.

Be curious . When you're in awe, you must to be open to hearing other people's stories , regardless what their backgrounds. Your curiosity will allow you to develop your empathy as you take the time to talk to people who you wouldn't have encountered in the first place.

Frame the right questions - What kind of questions you ask will affect the level of empathy you show. It is essential to ask the appropriate questions that relate to the topic under discussion.

How to make New Friends

It is likely that you will meet new people most of the times. It's important to acquire skills in how to begin to nurture and build new friendships. This section provides tips on how you can make new acquaintances.

Your fears are unfounded. Many people are afraid of the prospect of meeting strangers. They'll take a long time to consider what they'll say to their new friends and the impressions that new people will have about their new acquaintances. The idea of meeting new people can be a bit frightening. But, it's important to find out that your fear is not substantiated and only helping to stop new people from being introduced to your life.

Start small. If you're afraid of getting to know new people you'll get to socialize with and eventually become close friends with, it's recommended to start with your friends. It's crucial to start with your friends' friends as well as your acquaintances. You should also accept invitations to go out. Once you've started with individuals you're familiar with and trust, you'll start to build confidence in meeting people haven't met for all of your life.

Take a step out now - Now that you've strengthened your friendship bonds with your close friends It's time to get out and meet completely new people. You can achieve this by attending meetups, workshops and volunteering, going to events, parties, and many more. Meetups groups allow you to meet other people who share the same interests as yours. For instance, you could hold a gathering of people who are interested in cycling, or in online marketing. Workshops provide training opportunities for those interested in certain areas such as research. It is essential to know the time a workshop you're interested in will begin in order to be able to go and meet new people.

Begin by making the first move. First, greet someone by introducing yourself. Let the other person know your life story and give them the chance to share something else. First, do not get into a complex topic, but instead ask the participants questions like the topics they came across in the class.

Be open minded It is essential to be open in your eyes whenever you meet new people in the world and not make assumptions about them. It is important to allow some time pass before judging individuals. For instance, if you'd like to meet a person who is a lover of traveling to different places, but believes that the person you've had a conversation with doesn't, it is important to let them rest before you begin to judge them. You might be able to pique the interest of them and they'll start going out. At the same time it's important to let your heart open to the other person. It's about trusting them and believing you're good friends with them.

Know the person you're talking to - When you begin to build a relationship, it's crucial to be able to understand the other in order to build a lasting connection. You must learn about their activities as well as their interests, hobbies and other interests.

Chapter 7: A Good Conversation Guides: Things to Discuss

Engaging in small conversations to break up a tense silence or to get to know the person you're talking to can be challenging, especially if not very knowledgeable on how to do it. If you're still an inexperienced participant in small-talking and want to improve your skills in this field most likely among the first things you'll need to look into are the best small talk topics. This chapter will discuss the top topics to use to begin small-talk discussions and make them into smart conversations. There are also some helpful tips for success with them.

Foods

Most situations suitable to begin small-sized discussions include food. It is therefore advisable to bring up this topic when you're trying to start the conversation. You could, for instance, discuss how the food items served at a gathering look fantastic, and ask your guest what they would suggest. You could also make comments on the beautiful design of the food that he is eating, and then follow by mentioning where he purchased the food.

You can also start conversations by commenting on food items and then asking the method of preparation or potential ingredients. Food is something that a lot of people can agree on therefore, if you begin to open conversation on the subject, you'll likely get an answer.

Recommendations

It's never a bad idea to show a person a nice gesture at times. It's actually effective to begin conversations. Don't be shy to tell someone that there's something about them that makes you smile. For example, you could make a comment about her stunning brooch and add the question of where he acquired the item. You could also compliment his style.

It's not just focused on the physical appearance. Also, you may want to praise him/her for his talents for example, his ability to write a wonderful article or a view on a specific subject. Also, inform him that you admire his capacity to handle a variety of duties in a tranquil manner. This type of conversation can create an enduring bond due to its fact it mostly is focused on positive energy. You're sharing something positive about themselves, which could immediately help you connect with them and draw their attention.

Interests

It is also possible to start an informal conversation by speaking about possible interests you share. If, for instance, you're in a spot with film buffs You can ask a person in the vicinity whether they're also working in the film industry, or if he's an fan like you. This can give two and you something interesting to discuss.

If you're speaking to a teacher, you can inform him or her of your admiration by the work he does. Then, you can follow it by describing why you feel so passionate about teaching, and other advantages that come with being an educator. If you can tap into the interest of someone and showing them that you're also interested in it, you'll make someone new who's willing to chat with you about things.

A specific location or occasion the event you're attending

If you are looking to break the ice you're in a particular area or at a particular time, discuss something related to an event or situation. Be attentive and examine. Determine if there's something you should mention. One example is telling the person in front of you how great the space or the location is, or how amazing the food and services provide, and how well decorated the location is. When the one you're talking with is also impressed by what you've seen the venue, he'll probably reply, giving two of you something to talk about.

Pets

It is also possible to ask someone about their pets. Pets are typically the most frequent topic of people who are unable to discover something common to discuss. If you're a dog enthusiast in general you will find it simple to connect with others who are pet-lovers and. The best part about this is that you are able to be confident in initiating the conversation about this subject regardless of what pet that he loves, whether it's cats, dogs or birds, horses or even the wild. While some might get irritated by talking about your pet, remember the fact that asking about their pet is a good way of opening up to them and allowing them to be a bit of fun.

Current Situation

If you're hoping to become an expert at small talk and small talks, it might be helpful to find out more about the current happenings. Take a look at newspapers or catch the news on TV , so you can get a sense of current events happening in the society in the present. This will immediately give you an idea of what you can discuss. It's likely that your friends and family members know about this topic, too so speaking with them about it can quickly spark intelligent conversations.

You should be informed of what's happening in your area and around the world. The positive side is that now you can get important information about the news online. You can obtain them directly from trustworthy news websites or find them on social media. These online sources will help to keep you up-to-date, meaning you'll never be short of ideas while talking to people.

Weather

While the weather isn't a particularly interesting subject to discuss however, it's actually an interesting conversation starter that anyone can discuss. If, for instance, there were recent storms, you can discuss the weather. You could also make a comment on the pleasant weather, and then you can follow up with an inquiry about what he normally does in favorable weather.

Entertainment and arts

They include topics such as recent films and TV shows as well as popular music, books , or popular restaurants. Make sure you have prepared for these topics in case you plan to use them to start small discussions in the future. Learn about the latest trends in the entertainment and arts sector. Reading books can provide you with more information on this subject, which makes it easier to come up with something you could talk about.

Sports

These include topics such as your the teams you love bowl games, tournaments, as well as other sporting events. One of the advantages of this is that, even if you're not a fan of sports There's always something to talk about. In particular, for instance you could talk to about the reasons you don't like sports.

Another suggestion is to keep a log of sports that are played in particular seasons, like hockey, golf, football and soccer. It will be simpler to consider the most popular topics to discuss in small group discussions that relate to sports. If the Olympics are currently in progress for instance, you can be sure that everybody will be talking about it in the course of the conversation.

Family

A few people may speak to you through questions concerning your family. You might be asked whether you have sisters or brothers and how many people are in the family, if there are children in your family, how long the two of you married or in a relationship, etc. Be prepared for these kinds of topics and questions because people are likely to ask these questions in small conversations. It is also possible to reciprocate by asking them questions about their families.

Work

The workplace is a great subject for small-talks. Find out about the current position that the individual you're talking with and what he loves most about it. Don't be afraid to give information regarding your job and, in turn, you're likely to get asked about the same.

Travel destinations / Vacations

Another subject important to talk about is vacation or travel. The majority of people enjoy going to different places, so you should be prepared to discuss the topic if you're looking to have small conversations. If you frequent travel and are willing to talk about your thoughts and experiences from your past travels to anyone looking for information.

Ask them about their dream destination or their favorite place, and. Try asking for their suggestions. The majority of them will be more than willing to recommend a good spot to you, and will be happy to provide their expertise about it. This is a great method to turn your conversation into deeper conversations.

Apart from the topics already mentioned, other subjects you can successfully begin small discussions and keep the conversation going include hobbies, local news gossips, celebrity gossips, and so on. The great thing about these subjects is that they are both safe and low-risk so they're likely to get a positive reaction.

There's a less chance you'll fail when you're using these subjects since the majority of them are designed to engage with those around you, as well as allowing you to identify common ground.

Chapter 8: Learning the Art Of Small Talk

Small talk is designed to provide people with a chance to meet new people, and build connections to conversations about opportunities. If you are looking to make connections small talk is a great way to put people at ease, pulls participants into conversation and creates a relaxation zone that allows you to build a rapport with people. Here are some suggestions for mastering the art of making small conversation.

Create an informal chat. Sort topics you like engaging in conversation and can discuss with ease. Select topics that you aren't familiar with but would like to get to know more from others. My most popular topics are current events, such as the crude oil instance above. Tips: Avoid political issues or crises which could result in losing interest in the discussion.

Because the majority people don't want to talk or listen about the issues that arise in our lives or in the community.

Relax the listener. Let them feel relaxed and let them settle down and have fun in having a conversation in a relaxed manner with you. Be sure to avoid lecturing or making a lasting impression to your people listening. If you're in a the presence of a potential client It is recommended to approach for a meal that they can decide where they would like to take a bite. If they let you pick the location of the event Coffee shops are the most frequent and convenient place for informal meetings to meet and discuss about deals. Because of their quiet atmosphere that makes it easy to grasp the deal that is being made.

Be inquisitive. Curiousness increases your understanding and perception of things. You should be curious about who they as individuals, or as businessmen. However, too much curiosity could result in danger, so be cautious not to get caught up in the point where you make people uncomfortable or angry.

Learn to be a good listener. Pay attention more than you talk. The importance of listening with thought is not just small conversations. When you listen you are aware of what you should respond to establish a relationship with the person who is speaking. As you continue to listen,, the more knowledge and understanding you acquire from the messenger.

Be attracted. Your enthusiasm can cause other people want to speak openly with you. Interacting with others is often the best way to let them know their ideas. As an example, you can participate to the conversation. If people want to speak with you, you can respond with a word or phrase.

Seek out the common areas of interest. To continue the conversation give topics to discuss until you find something that interests the person listening and you. If someone does not respond to your approach immediately Do not assume that the person isn't at all. Keep trying. If your topic is of interest for the other, they may accept. Sharing experiences or ideas with other people to stimulate the conversation.

Think about your future. Small talk is a good basis for relationships and a network. You can develop an intimate bond of knowledge of connectedness and connection with others. The network you build can benefit you in a variety of ways. The chapter 5 we will discuss how network can assist you with your career and business.

Icebreakers

Icebreaker can help you in becoming a good conversationalist. Look over the list of questions for icebreakers below and pledge to at least use a few of them in any subsequent conversation. If you think you'll forget them take a note of them and put them in your purse, and revisit them before engaging in a conversation. If you're unable to remember them during the moment, you should take a break for a few minutes and head to a secure area to look at the list.

SOCIAL ICEBREAKERS

Please tell me the very first game you've played.

Do you find that the internet helps your to improve your life?

What is your top singer or artist/video game persona? Why?

Write about a memorable teacher you have had.

Tell me about a film or book you that you've watched or book that you've read many times.

What is your top restaurant? Why?

Do you have a view about the movie, cafe or event?

Tell me about the best 3 vacation tips you've used.

What's your top activity?

If you were able to relive any moment of your life What would that be?

Let me know about the family you have.

Tell us about the most frightening moment of your life.

What's a typical day for you?

Tell me about the most memorable moments in your life.

What was the atmosphere like in the town in which you grew up?

From all the meals you've eaten, the places you've been to / films you've seen I'd like to know which one that you enjoyed the most.

What did you learn about draw, sing, cook or play?

What is your most loved family custom that you particularly love?

What is the one thing you would most like to own? Why?

What do you want to return as the next time?

Business ICEBREAKERS

Do you know anyone who can help me _____?

Define the way and time in your life has a direct impact on your work.

How did you think of this idea?

What are the most significant changes you've observed in your company since its beginning?

Write about the most unusual thing you've had to deal with in your job.

What inspired you to get started in this profession, industry or field of study?

What is it that separates your company from other companies?

What is the most difficult aspect you do?

How does the Internet affected your work or your profession?

What do you think are the next trends for your company?

What strategies have you discovered to be the most effective method to promote your company?

Tell us about your most memorable job experience.

What advice would you offer to a potential client who is just beginning with your business?

What was the most successful firm you've ever worked with? What made you decide to leave?

What attracted you to research, marketing, or training?

What are you most excited about in your job or career?

What exactly does your company or create / provide a service?

Give a brief description of some of the obstacles of your profession.

Non verbal Communication matters

When we interact with others without conscious thought, we transmit messages by using our bodies. This type of communication is known as non-verbal communication. However, no matter what we do we can't escape the subconscious message we transmit when making small talk, regardless of whether we cease transmitting messages. So, instead of trying to avoid it, we can make use of it to make small talk more effective.

Eye Contact - Begin conversation by making eye contact, and then presenting the other person with a warm and inviting smile. This eases tension and shows the person you're willing to discuss the topic. As per Don Gabor,, the author of "Talking in Confidence for the Shy," declare that looking at someone for between five and 10 seconds indicates curiosity and is considered to be friendly. However, never gaze directly into another's eyes for too long, which can could make someone be uncomfortable.

Expressions of facial and gestures - the way you move and look, pay attention and respond tells someone if you're in the mood or are not. The way you look and gestures tell that you are honest, and also how well you listen. If your body movements and facial expressions are consistent with what you're communicating, it enhances the transparency, trust and trust. If they don't, it can cause tension disbelief, suspicion, and confusion.

The body's posture or movements Consider how you look at other people in regards to how they sit, walk, or stand, this are what body movement communicates. The manner in which we move and how we post sends a message to our receiver. If you're engaged in conversation, always be sure to stand, walk or be seated in a way that is appropriate.

Touching - Every when you touch something, you send an overwhelming message to the person who is receiving it. For instance, if you make a gesture with care, you convey a sense of love to the receiver.Thus by introducing yourself with a bit with a handshake sends the receiver a the impression that you're serious and are interested in an exchange.

Space - Have you felt uncomfortable in a circumstance where someone is sitting or standing at a distance? This is referred to as space communication. It transmits signal based on the distance between the sender and receiver. If you're near someone and you find that the person is dispersing with you, that could mean that the person and you have problems. If you do engage in an attempt to talk, ensure that your distance from the receiver will make him or her feel relaxed.

Chapter 9: Creative Strategies to Begin Small Talks

If you've figured out the potential topics you can discuss, it's the time to determine what you need to do to get it done and start the discussion. Be aware that, even the best you know about potential topics for small talk topics but you'll be unable to pull it off if aren't sure how to convey the message. This chapter will discuss several of the helpful techniques that can aid you in this phase.

Ask open-ended questions.

Many people like to discuss themselves, and engaging in this type of conversation is the best way to begin small conversations and keep the conversation moving. Questions that are open to discussion require explanations instead of a straightforward yes or no answer. They typically begin with is, who, what you can answer them. They also include where, what, and when. Closed questions are, however begin with the words are/am/is have and do. One example of an open-ended questions would be what kind of songs do you enjoy the most and what is it? This usually requires an explanation and you're able to get just a simple "yes or no" as an answer. Because there's a reason to respond, you are able to extend the conversation.

Recall earlier discussions

If you're talking with someone you've spoken to previously, it's ideal to keep an idea of the topics that you've talked about prior to. It is possible to continue talking about the same topic. Examples include an unpleasant news story he relayed to you, an idea which he's working towards or a recent accomplishment of your child. In addition to giving you some ideas on what you can discuss and how to approach it, it could help the other person feel more comfortable, as this is a sign that you're paying attentively to what he's saying. It shows him how attentive of a listener and how much you value the issues and experiences the other person shared with you. It can also encourage him to create a bond.

Ask him questions that he will easily respond to

In order to successfully start small conversations and make sure that conversations continue moving, ensure that you make sure which the other person is not going to have a difficult in answering or responding to. Be aware that there are certain types of questions which are difficult to respond to. If you're looking to get someone's attention, ask simple and intriguing questions that they will be eager to answer. This will help to ensure that conversations be more enjoyable and flow more easily and make the two of you feel more at ease.

Be aware

It's not a good idea to ask someone a question without thinking about whether or not they're willing to discuss the subject or topic that you're looking for. When you ask him questions ensure that it's not invasive. It shouldn't be related to issues they don't wish to talk about. For example some people may be angry or upset in the event that you ask them to discuss things that impact their personal lives. This includes weight, insufficient qualifications or abilities, relationships issues, etc. Be mindful and sensitive. Avoid discussing things that could cause them to lose people's privacy, or create a feeling of guilty about their own self-esteem.

Mention the name of the person you're talking with periodically

In addition to aiding you in remembering his name, it's an effective method to show gratitude and to ensure that he feels comfortable. Making reference to him by his name will help make the conversation more intimate, personal and authentic. This can create more connections Don't be amazed by the conversation you started ended up being a more intelligent deeper, more meaningful one.

Stay engaged

Be sure to not appear bored while you are talking to anyone. You want him to feel that you're really involved in the conversation you've started and are interested in what he's talking about.

Make him feel that to continue the conversation. Keep your eyes on him equally. Make sure that your interest remains engaged, rather than trying to regress from yourself. This is crucial in order to maintain an enjoyable and relaxed conversation, and ensure that it goes on for.

The advantage of staying engaged throughout the entire time you talk to one another is that it can provide you with ideas for subjects to discuss during your subsequent small talk and conversations. This is particularly true in the event that you'll be talking to the same person over and over again. This can provide you with a clue about the topics you can possibly talk regarding, for instance, wanting to know the status of some aspect of his life.

Be yourself

In small discussions it's not necessary to pretend to be like you're speaking to someone else as this will only cause you to feel uncomfortable. Do what you are comfortable with. React to situations according to the way you usually respond. Smile and laugh naturally every when someone comes up with a joke or humorous comment. Be careful not to force laughter you might be alarming him. Smile and smile naturally. You are yourself, and you'll most likely express these actions naturally instead of looking awkward and forced.

Don't be concerned about the pauses

It's not a problem in the event of pauses following the discussion of an issue. The great thing about pausing is that you can effectively use them to switch the topic. They also function as an opportunity to take a quick break or a breather, and then re-energize the conversation. There's nothing to worry about , unless the silence and pause are already long enough. Do not stress yourself so long as you allow yourself for a bit or simply move on to the next topic, you're fine.

Don't be afraid of getting personal

This is a great idea, provided that you decide beforehand if the other party is open to discussing things that are personal to them. The benefit of becoming more intimate and with the permission of the other person is that you have an opportunity to connect to him quicker. You will quickly become familiar with him, making it simpler to establish an emotional connection. Certain topics that are safe even though they are a bit personal, that you could chat with him about could be his favourite book, his preferred sports team, his favorite hobbies and interests, as well as the holiday he is most excited about.

Ask follow-up questions

When you've begun the conversation, make certain to be attentive to the responses of your friend. This can be a big help in weaving great follow-up questions. Follow-up questions can keep the conversation running. Be sure to aren't too invasive in order to not annoy him. Your questions must be answered by something which he feels comfortable in.

Be careful not to make your conversation your partner uncomfortable, too. Be attentive to his responses whether they are spoken or in non-verbal form. It's also recommended to be more polite when you respond to those who are uneasy or uncomfortable in the presence of. When the individual you're speaking to appears uninterested in sharing information or information or appears to be uninterested, avoid talking to them for too long.

When asking follow-up questions are crucial to keep the conversation moving, you must know when to end the conversation. Beware of asking too many questions if the person begins to lose interest.

Chapter 10: Listening, and Knowledge

Listening

Listening is a vital ability. It's a function performed by our brains and ears, and is performed involuntarily, however most of us don't take the time to spend time listening.

There is no communication that is complete without being able to listen.

Within an organizational structure research has shown that employees are able to spend 45 percent of their working hours listening.

Based on Tom Peters, a leading management expert listening is a crucial management and leadership ability. It is especially crucial for students, since they are spending the majority of their time watching lectures.

Listening is defined as: the act of receiving, interpreting , and responding to a message from an individual speaker.

Hearing and listening

Hearing is entirely dependent on the ears. It's a physical action. Hearing is the simple vibration of sound waves in the eardrum, then the firing of electro-chemical signals to the brain.

Listening is, however is a choice made by the individual. It involves a conscious effort to pay attention and understanding what you hear. It requires conscious effort to understand the sounds, understand how words are used, and respond in response to the information. The understanding of sounds is a mental action that depends on the comprehension of the person listening, and also his attitudes towards the sender and the message. A negative attitude towards the sender or speaker can impact the listening process to a large extent.

Listening styles

Appreciative Listening: Listening to music for the purpose of gaining aesthetic pleasure. E.g. listening to music, comedian , or entertainer

Emphatic Listening: Listening to offer moral and emotional support is described as emphatic listening. E.g. parents listening to their children's issues in order to offer moral and emotional support to them.

Comprehensive Listening: This is typically required in classrooms, in which students are required to listen to the lecturer in order to learn and comprehend the material given.

Critical Listening: If the goal in listening is take or deny a message, or to evaluate it critically Critical listening is necessary. E.g. when you go through a book with the goal of writing a review you are using your critical listening skills.

When you're engaging in conversation when you're talking about small talk, you could utilize any of the four kinds of listening to ensure that you are able to keep the person talking. If the other person tells an amusing story, you enjoy the moment; when he talks about some of the issues he has as parent, you provide assistance; when she wants to be understood in a way, you pay attention to her and when he needs suggestions on how to proceed then you listen attentively.

It is possible that you require to display all these traits when you are listening to someone's small conversation.

Characteristics of a good listener

If you're engaged in a conversation with a friend What are the characteristics you exhibit as a person who listens?

Active listening requires an enormous amount of effort however it's not difficult. Some guidelines are provided below to ensure that you are active and efficient listening.

Being non-evaluative If you're an active participant, your spoken and non-verbal behavior will indicate your speaker is heard and is understood. You don't evaluate the speaker based on the thoughts and feelings that he is able to convey. As a listener take note of the characteristics of the ideas that are delivered to you by your speaker. Your behavior conveys of the person speaking that you trust the speaker without making any judgments, the right or wrong whether acceptable or not, or not.

Paraphrasing: If it is your intention to clarify something it is possible to take the words of the speaker spoken and ask the speaker if you've been able to understand it or not. E.g.

"As I've gathered you'd like to share ..."

"Do you mean ...?"

"So do you want to claim that ..."

Reflecting Implications: In order to reflect the implications of your thoughts, you need be able to think beyond the context of the information the speaker present and be awed by the speaker's thoughts and their ideas and what they can lead you to. The goal of the listener is to show enthusiasm and excitement by nodding by speaking, thus providing positive feedback.

Reflecting on Hidden feelings Reflecting Hidden Feelings: Sometimes, you'll be required to explore more than the words and emotions that the speaker has presented and may need to uncover the hidden emotions, intentions, as well as opinions or values that the speaker is experiencing.

Inviting Other Contributions You may not be able to comprehend or hear the speaker correctly. Respond by asking the speaker to provide more details. If you'd like to ask the speaker to elaborate on his topic, you can pose open-ended questions instead of a straightforward "Yes" or "No". Avoid asking probing or direct questions directed at the speaker. Inquiring questions that open up can create a more supportive and secure environment that helps keep the communication flowing. Make sure that your comments are concise and simple to comprehend. Be aware that when you are doing most of the talking, then you likely aren't paying attention.

The most effective way to LISTEN is to remain silent. Silent and Listen share identical letters and spelling.

Responding Non-Verbally: You may prove that you're an avid listener taking particular postures or sending signals to convey your enthusiasm for the words of the speaker. Certain non-verbal responses include

A few times, the head may nod

Maintain eye contact with the speaker.

Lean your body slightly toward the speaker.

Tips to Improve Listening

You can become a great listener by gaining a desire to listen

Get clarifications

Don't interrupt or complete the speaker's sentences, or frighten the speaker by asking inappropriate or trick questions.

Utilize affirmative prompting using non-verbal and verbal means

Be aware of your body speech

Paying Attention

Small talk is about paying complete attention to the person speaking or the person with whom you are speaking during the conversation.

You are often listening to various types of communications in a way that is not conscious. E.g. at a restaurant, while eating at a restaurant, we can listen to various sounds, such as the sound of the programmes on television, the sound of people talking, etc. It is not listening actively.

You must be alert in order to follow a program on TV or to listen to people speak.

The question is "How do you build the capacity to listen to people attentively and attentively?"

Unintentional listening can be very damaging to communication since distortion sets in. Unintentional listening is also unproductive.

It is your duty as the listener to display awe in the speaker and speech through proper expressions, being alert and asking questions about the speech when necessary. If you do this, you'll inspire the speaker to communicate his thoughts clearly and enthusiastically. If there's a look of boredom on his or his or her face, it could deter the speaker.

You can increase your proficiency in this field by listening to commentary on radio or television. Pay attention to the main idea as well as the supporting ideas, and on the digressions that occur, if they are within the commentary. You can also record the essence of what you heard. This will definitely aid in improving your listening skills.

In order to be active in listening, it's not enough simply to listen towards the speakers. Also important is the physical characteristics of the speaker / person. This includes the appearance of the speaker facial expressions, body movement and posture. These are as crucial in conveying meaning as words used in the speech.

Generallyspeaking, the body language, or non-verbal communication is voluntary, and therefore more authentic. As a listener must pay close focus on the physical signals that the speaker is delivering to determine the authenticity and credibility of the speech.

As as a listener, when you notice that the speaker has a negative attitude, you are likely to avoid listening because you are not a fan of criticism.

To be a shrewd and competent listener, it is essential to seek out a legitimate motive for your criticism, and also what's triggered the speaker's discontent. Receptive and constructive approach to criticism can result in your own improvement. You are more likely to hear the messages that are appealing or pleasing to you. But you must also be able to be equally interested in speeches that include messages that are interesting to the speaker.

Resolving Distractions

If you're engaged in an informal conversation there is a chance that you're distracted by the sound of your phone or the sound that might be coming from outside and so on. In such situations you have to manage distractions.

As you develop active listening abilities You should learn to stay clear of physical distractions and focus on the message. A beautiful face or the perfume's sweet scent could be the cause of distraction. But, as a discerning listener, it is essential to practice a lot of mental discipline in order to stay focussed on the message being delivered from the presenter.

In most cases, after a time of intense listening it becomes exhausting and lose enthusiasm for the message.

You must work to keep your focus on the words and the content.

Many times, the cause of these problems is "brain timing". On average, you talk about 130-150 words per minute. In contrast, your brain is able of absorbing 600-700 phrases per minute. Therefore, your mind is likely to wander when the speech becomes monotonous. To get over this issue it is important to be aware to anticipate what the speaker is going to speak the next time. If the speaker's predictions are accurate, then your curiosity in the speech will be renewed. This will allow you to remember the speech more easily and constantly review what was said before.

If you are focused on fragments of the message, you are not paying the complete attention. Sometimes interrupting the speaker and not taking in the whole message is not a good decision to make.

If you pay attention make sure you don't make a quick judgment about the message until the speaker is completed his or her speech. Effective listening can only happen when you listen attentively to the whole speech.

Always make an effort to listen to the message with a positive outlook. If you're pretentious you'll show your attention through unnatural postures such as sitting with your hands on your chin or bending too much to suggest that you're paying close concentration to the message even though your brain is absent. You aren't aware of which speaker talking about. Effective listening is not something that comes effortlessly; it takes a lot of effort from your side to pay close attention. As a listener , you need concentration and mental strength to focus on the speaker's words and also the non-verbal signals that indicate communication such as the way you move, your gesture, eye contact , facial expressions, as well as other signs.

Sometimes, even noise may cause distraction. It is important to learn to block out or divert attention from such noise, and concentrate on the speaker.

Imagine that you approach your mentor to discuss your issues and find him constantly working at his computer or his mobile phone, and he doesn't pay much attention to you. Would you want to do that?

Absolutely not! It is important to have a place suitable for you, so that your teacher is able to fully listen to your complaints, grievances and grievances. Listening with a sense of purpose is crucial in this instance. It will allow you to let go of emotional tensionsand enhance the atmosphere.

I think I've explained in detail the importance of listening to small conversations. It's not only about listening, it's also about your body expressions, postures, and gestures indicate whether you are listening to the speaker or not.

Knowledge

Alongside the listening skills mentioned in the preceding section that are crucial to be able to effectively engage with others Small Talk, you should be aware of a range of subjects.

It doesn't mean you must have a degree in all disciplines. For e.g. an insurance broker might experienced in sports but might not be comfortable with subjects related to rocket science and space exploration.

However, does this mean the broker must remain his distance when he encounters scientists in space and fails to know what he does? No!

What I am trying to convey is that if show an interest in the subject and keep your ears and eyes open, you'll learn more about a wide range of topics and be an important contributor to Small Talk.

Now the question is: how do you acquire the knowledge?

The only way to learn is through reading . This includes a wide range of magazines, books periodicals, fiction, and non-fiction. More you learn, the greater your perspective becomes. And you'll be able to make use of the knowledge acquired to impress others.

You can also utilize many other sources of information to increase your knowledge such as reading blogs, e-books, emagazines and more. to increase your understanding.

Journals and trade publications are another way to gain the knowledge of a particular field.

When you acquire information by staying abreast of the most recent developments in different fields, you'll be able impress others by your knowledge. It is not necessary to have a deep expertise, but it is enough for you to participate on Small Talk with a variety of people.

If you talk to people in small groups it is possible to learn more through conversations with others who have more information about the subject, which in turn, will expand your horizons.

The more you participate in small discussions the more confidence and understanding you'll acquire; and you will impress others by your confidence, expertise and ability to communicate.

Do you wish to be a part of the group who possess these talents and influence people? I'm betting you'd like to improve these skills and make people feel special. If you follow the suggestions I mentioned earlier You will be in the right direction to impress people with your knowledge as well as confidence and skills in conversation.

Chapter 11: Conversations with Others

As a painter has his brushes and paints and a writer has ink and quill, so you as a conversationalist use your ears, tongue and your body as a instrument.

A successful conversationalist should be able to communicate with others, take in other people's conversations and then present himself in a professional manner by using body language.Most times the best conversations don't depend on the amount of information you are aware of, but on how you convey your message, pay attention to other people and then present yourself to people you're speaking to.

However, having a wide range of topics is an effective tool to master conversation.Below are a few of the most frequently asked questions you can utilize to aid.

Conversation topics that are appropriate for conversations

Weather.Weather is usually a great starter.It is one of the things that will likely be common between you and those who you're chatting with.To keep the conversation going by sharing your story of what happened in a specific weather.However the topic of weather topics can become boring.Keep your conversation brief, unless the weather changes during the conversation.

The food you eat or meals.These are often the most popular items to have during conversations at an party.Complimenting the food may spark the conversation. By comparing it with someone else's or the food served at a restaurant could help it grow.Sharing your experience about the food may also be a way to work.

Work.Talking about work can be a great topic to spark conversation. Learning about the work of the other person can spark the conversation.Knowing what transpired at the course of work, or working on at the same place, or admiration for the job can help keep the conversation going for an extended period of time.

Hobbies.Talking about your interests can be a way to change the conversation, however it is tricky.Hobby is an intimate topic.Unless you are familiar with the person you are talking to, you will have to create a pretext for making the change in subject subtle.You could begin by connecting your interest to any of the other subjects.

For instance, if it's sunny outside then you can use the phrase, "It is a nice time to play a game of soccer.Do you enjoy soccer too?"You are able to continue conversations from there.If you're talking to someone else and they say yes, you can talk about soccer briefly bit.Then you can find the right time to inquire about the other activity he enjoys.

Politics.Politics is not a good starter for a conversation.It can be a good topic for a conversation.However, you need to be careful.Conversations about politics grow only when the parties have contrary views.It becomes boring if you share the same view.If you do not share the same views, the topic may get out of hand and the conversation may end up in a disagreement.Thus, make sure not to insist that the other party should change his view.Just present your view and respect his. If you agree with the opinion, you should try changing the subject after you have made your argument.

Children.This is a fun discussion for parents as well as grandparents.If you're an adult or grandparent you are likely to be able to talk, listen and talk about mishaps and mischiefs of your children. ones.Just be sure to not make a point of comparing your children, or your sweet chat will turn sour.If you don't own children, then you might need to alter the subject or even leave yourself out.

Current events.These include political and featured reports, news and even shows business.These are excellent ideas to follow up on the weather topic.Everyone can have something to say about current events.The subjects can shift from one event to the next without having to force it.However you must restrict the subject to not changing constantly.Some people in the group might think it's a waste of time.

Questions that may not be appropriate for an open conversation

The topics that are personal might not be appropriate for an conversation. They are not appropriate for an conversation.As as much as is possible don't bring it up during the course of a conversation.Some of the topics include:

Marriage.Unless you're taking part in a marriage workshop and you are not a married person, it is advised to avoid discussing the subject in a public conversation.Some strangers could join with you and the marital troubles might be exposed to them. If you're discussing the pleasures of marriage and those who are struggling in their marriage could be annoyed.

It is also about the fidelity, loyalty , and marriage life of those who aren't part of the conversation. Generic marital topics like laws on marriage, weddings, right age to marry can be a safe topic in a conversation.However, they are often boring.

Sexual life or love life.Your love life or that of the people who are part of the discussion are private matters.It is recommended to have the subject addressed in personal or private discussion as it can be a sensitive subject for certain people in the group.

Grievances.Personal grievances, or ones that are related to your job are better addressed in private matters.Sharing your grievance in a casual conversation could hurt your relationship with your employer or colleagues.

How to Talk in a Conversation

Conversation is a process that takes place through speaking.If the speaker fails to follow this aspect, the conversation will fail.

Here are some tips for how to talk to others during the course of a conversation.

Talk to people with a tone and modulation which makes your person appear relaxed and at ease.If you speak with the tone of a quiet discussion, another participant might think you're not interested.If you speak with high-pitched tone you could make the other party be tempted to quit the conversation due to their ears hurt, or you are attracting the attention of the other guests.

Talk with ease. There are times when you may misspell some of the words when talking.You may be awkward or embarrassed due to this mistake.However when you be focused on being a flawless speaking style, you might appear rigid and boring.Other people who prefer an informal conversation, rather than an articulate one, might not stick around long enough to continue in the conversation. Speaking in conversation does not mean that a person must be eloquent.Articulation may help in a conversation, but it is not a prerequisite.Hence, speak with ease.

Engage in conversation with enthusiasm.Many people talk only with those whom they are inclined to talk with them. Your enthusiasm should be displayed through your body expression and facial expression.Even even if you sound enthusiastic about the subject, however, your body doesn't convey that excitement and the other person may find it difficult to relate to you.But don't interpret your your body expressions. It could cause the other person to lose focus on your remarks.

Do not declare conclusions.Conclusive sentences may not give the other party the chance to comment or give their opinions.Conclusions are presented in reports and lectures.In conversations, you should only speak your opinion and not conclude.

"The clouds look to be dark. It's going to rain today."This is an assertion. The other party has no choice but to go with your conclusion. However, if you state it such as, "The clouds seem dark. Do you think it's going to be raining today?"Here you're giving an opportunity for the conversation to expand.

Be sure to address all parties.If you're speaking to two or more people it is essential to engage in the conversation with everyone members of them.Talking to one person and not addressing the other could be a snare to the others.They could end up abruptly leaving the conversation. The best method to avoid this is to select a subject that is common to the majority of parties.It can keep the conversation lively and enjoyable.

Hearing the Other Parties

Conversations develop through listening.It is a method to pay focus to someone talking.Listening can give you the chance to accurately respond to the conversation and keep the conversation going.

The ability to listen well is crucial in a conversation.The comments made during the conversation are typically short and clear to the point.If the concise and brief message is misinterpreted due to insufficient listening, it could cause confusion or cause an argument that is heated.

Below are some helpful tips for listening effectively in an exchange.

Be curious and curious. There are instances when you might not know much about the topic. Some people are prone to be bored and walk away. But, if you're trying to become a great speaker, do not leave. Instead be interested in the topic. Asking questions is a part of the conversation as well.

Listening does not happen through the ears only. It requires participation of the mind. If you're not sure about the topic the person in question can ask questions to learn more about the subject. It is important to listen to the ideas , not just the words to be able to pose questions that are sensible and increase the discussion.

But, it is important to be careful not to ask too many questions as the conversation could be perceived as an interview.Or more importantly, others might conclude that you're ignorant.

Visualize the words or the statement that the other party makes. Imagine how the person speaking is saying.You might be able to know what he's trying to convey since you are able to see his message clearly. This will enable you to react with a sense of urgency or build an interest in the topic.

The speaker should feel at ease.A skilled conversationalist will allow the other person to complete his remarks prior to asking questions, or making an comment.If you interrupt frequently the speaker, it could cause him to feel uncomfortable or , even more, offended.Also it is not advisable to immediately change the topic if you aren't sure about the current topic.It could be a snare to the speaker.

Watch your eyes too.Ears are the only way to hear words.Sometimes the words aren't the message, but rather an expression from the speaker.Thus it is important to observe the manner in which the speaker is speaking for a better understanding of what he's trying to say or to determine his motivation to the topic.

Eye contact with the speaker can make him feel relaxed and conveys your interest.However be aware that maintaining eye contact is beneficial however, staring at the speaker at the speaker's features is not.A attentive listener should refrain from looking at the speaker's features when speaking. This can make him feel uneasy and anxious.

Be mindful not to distract yourself while listening to an speaker.When you hear someone talking, pay him the complete attention he requires. Avoid taking your eyes off to another party.The person speaking may think your bored, or disinterested.He could interrupt the conversation and leave.

How to present yourself in the course of a conversation

If someone is naturally charismatic, he can easily engage in an conversation.For those who weren't gifted with this talent but, it's something they must learn.Here are some suggestions to make up for any lack of charisma.

You should look pleasant.One doesn't have to dress in a formal way to appear nice. Sometimes, a smile can help a person appear pleasant and approachable.A person is able to engage in conversation with someone new simply by smiling. Others would be more likely to keep talking with you, if you appear friendly.

Be confident.Conversation can easily end if the other party is not confident enough to present a reply or a comment.When you are not confident, you may choose to simply answer in few words.Replies like "Yes" or "No" will not make the conversation grow.You should present your justification or opinion about your answer.This will show your confidence.Do not be afraid if your opinion is different from the others.Convincing them to see your point of allowing them to convince you to see theirs is a good ground on whicn to make the conversation grow.

Don't do huge reactions when the conversation demands it.Some listeners might make big reactions in order to show that they're engaged in the conversation.Big reactions can cause the conversation to appear fake.Reactions must be fluid and appropriate to the context. Be careful not to laugh loudly and jumping around, or, even worse, striking the person in front of you to prove how enjoyable or funny the conversation.

Be aware about the conversation's other party.Conversation is in two-way communication.It is not an unintentional monologue.You must not steal the spotlight completely on you. Let other participants have their own spotlights within the conversation.

Make sure you are polite.Parties in a discussion aren't equally intelligent or funny.If someone else asks to clarify the conversation and you are polite, give an clarification.If you were the one to make jokes and they are not humorous, you must smile with respect and never mention that the joke isn't funny.Instead try to assist and make the joke fun.

Also, be aware about your body language.Avoid talking with your shoulders in a slump or by placing your hands placed on your chest. Others may believe that you're too exaggerating or are pressured into the conversation. If you are listening, try not to shake you knees, fiddling with your hands, or looking at your watch.The person who is speaking may feel that you're disinterested.He might also feel uneasy about himself. They could also believe that you are rude.

Additional suggestions on how you can have fun and enhance your conversations

Make sure you have knowledge.A person is never absent in a conversation if they are aware of many topics.A extensive knowledge of general info, music, and current events can help it possible to have a long and fascinating conversations.

Prepare yourself for the people you may meet.If you're planning to attend an event and you are likely to meet certain friends, it is possible to think about what will occur at the party. This way you can anticipate responses or remarks, particularly when your friend makes the conversation seem boring.

Create a joke about specific topics.Jokes can be excellent for ice breakers.A conversationalist must have at least two jokes in his sleeve to provide laughter in the conversation, and to break frozen ice.

Chapter 12: What to Begin With Small Talk

It is sometimes difficult for you to begin having small discussions. While it may seem easy in a conversation, it's going to become physically daunting. When you try to talk to someone , but they won't respond or someone will come up to you and you are unable to respond. These are common situations in the beginning of conversations. You will need to improve your social skills to be able to have small conversations.

The next chapter in this series will will look at the different strategies you must take in order to engage in small discussions with strangers.

Hone your social skills

The first thing you'll need to complete before beginning to have a chat or chat is to develop your social abilities. It is not enough to just take the conversation casually and then talk to someone before you start. They may think you're a fool. It is important to think about the way you speak, tone, and your voice modulation and also improve your ability to present. If you are approached by someone wearing casual attire, they may hesitate before making a move to speak to you. You must ensure that you're presentable and that you smell good. Begin by conducting an experiment with a friend and ask them to assist you to develop your social skills to become more friendly.

Break the Ice

When you've honed your skills, you will need to look for or locate people you'd like to engage in a short chat with. You can't just randomly go through the streets choose a person, walk up to them and tell them, "Hi". Most likely, they won't reply in any way. Go to your local mall and search for people who you think would be a good conversationalist. Begin to approach them with confidence and start talking to them. It is important to make sure to break the ice so that the person you are talking to will instantly take a liking to your character. Keep in mind that the first impression can be an impression that lasts forever, so you must try to be the best you can in the beginning of your interaction.

Introduce yourself

The next step will be to present yourself. Once you have done that you must remain in a straight line and spread your left hand. Don't extend your left, because it could send an incorrect message. Provide them with your full name and tell them what you do. Do not begin by divulging too many details , like your address , the location of your office as well as other details. It will only scare people and making them question what the point is of divulging so much details. You can ask them questions about them in a gentle manner and then encourage them to reveal their name. Keep it polite and avoid being too insistent on them.

Start by making it simple

After you have exchanged pleasantries, you can begin to have simple conversations. Don't begin with your most intelligent self because it could cause you to appear as overbearing and boastful. It is best to reduce your tone by a couple of notches, and start with a comment on something you and your partner can both see such as the decor of the mall or a book that could be stored away. Choose topics that are general but not overly specific. Discuss current issues. Since it's a small talk, engage in small conversations and quickly proceed to the next step.

Be yourself

If you are having a conversation with strangers, it's very easy to get lost. It is tempting to brag about yourself, and actually, share false information about yourself to impress on someone else. However, if you do that you will impact you negatively. It will be difficult maintain a conversation with someone who is lies and will result in you needing to cut off the conversation and move away.

Then build upon the casual conversation

When you are done discussing the things you observe, switch the subject and try to keep them entertained. However, for each discussion, ensure that the conversations are brief and relevant. Be sure not to stray from subjects excessively or make up abstract topics just for the fun of it. You must be able to identify a connection between the subjects and then move into the next subject.

Make a decision about the future

When you've finished your conversation, you need to determine the direction the relationship. It is up to you to determine if you enjoy the person enough to maintain an ongoing relationship or if you don't have any interest in any of that. You have the option of deciding whether you had a pleasant chat with them, and appear like great people to include in your circle of friends, or if you would prefer to say goodbye to them and go on. If you're not sure, then simply go away.

Mutually agreed upon

If you choose to establish a an ongoing relationship with the person you are interested in, then request their contact number or offer them your number. Make sure they're also keen on staying connected to you and that you aren't imposing your will on them. Ask them if like to remain in contact with you, and then provide them your contact information. Don't give your email address to them.

Stay on top of things

When you have made friends with them, make sure you do not let them go away. Plan to meet up occasionally for a social gathering and engage in small discussions. Be sure to only have a short amount of time for example, no more than 30 minutes at every meeting before heading back. Do not make them meet with you or send them a lot of mails or messages. Instead, slow down and let them send you a message or respond to you.

Get moving

When you make your first acquaintance You must look for the next. You can't stop at only one, and you will need to keep making small talk with strangers. You probably won't want to keep in touch with everyone, and you may encounter a few that can cause you to become angry or frustrated. You can ignore such people and just keep in contact with the top people.

Chapter 13: The Best Way to Begin A Conversation

If you've got many ideas for how to make friends and make people feel comfortable, it's time to begin improving your conversation skills. Keep in mind that talking about small things does not hurt anyone and it may even help people feel more relaxed more comfortable and less isolated. There is no reason to be anxious, uncomfortable or self-conscious to begin a conversation.

When you are beginning the conversation it is important to follow a few important guidelines you have be aware of. This way things will go well for you. In addition, it's helpful to have a few tips to guide you in the right direction while you work on your social abilities. These are the initial steps you should be aware of when having an interaction:

Begin with the person who is the most "approachable person"

When you're at an event for business or social or even on an elevator you should try to identify the most approachable one in the crowd. You'll be able to identify this person is since they are the one who has a conversation with you. They are not engaged in a conversation or working on some other task. This could be someone who's at a loss and could be a bit uncomfortable due to the presence of the other people in the vicinity. That's the person which you can start an exchange of words.

There are many people who are fascinating and welcoming however there are those who do not like being greeted so you need to be the one to take initiative and greets them with a hello. When you enter a room begin to look around and observe those who are standing or sitting by themselves. Do not be hesitant; instantly look at them and smile. If they smile back, you immediately have someone to speak to. The most approachable people are active listeners because they feel gratified to have someone take the time to make them feel at ease.

In order to break the ice with someone who is friendly Here are a few suggestions of statements you could test (or you could develop your own along these ideas). Make sure you ask questions like "why" and "how"?

This is such a beautiful day! What's a great idea to do on an event like this?

I believe that the food is delicious here! Which do you prefer the most?

It was a great film/show/program! Do you like it?

I'm completely confused! Please help me?

*Your jeans, dress or shoes appear chic! Where do you go to shop?

The flowers look very fresh! Are you aware of ways to keep them looking that fresh?

What a gorgeous house. What can you do to make sure everything is organized?

I'm very excited about my new supervisor. Do you have any thoughts on what his management style is?

Find out the name of the person and then keep it in mind

Making sure to mention names of people you're talking with every once in a while and with a sincere tone when you talk to them is an essential aspect. In the beginning, make sure you are focusing on the person's name and face and do not dwell on what you'll need to say or other information. It can help when you repeat the names once the person is presented to you. It is then that you should think of a response.

If you've misplaced their name or got distracted when he or she first introduced you to them, don't be shy about asking to know it again. Simply state, "I'm sorry, but I'm not certain if I did not know your full name." It's better than to continue the whole conversation and not know the name, or, even worse, use a different name for them.

If you meet an old friend and couldn't remember the person's name any longer it is possible to ask, "I'm really sorry, but I've lost your name. Would you mind reminding me?" The great thing with this approach is that you don't need to worry about staying away from certain individuals simply because you can't remember their names.

Another tip Avoid calling people by their name (unless they request it). For instance, if a person introduces his name by the name of "Joseph," avoid calling him "Joe". If the name of someone cannot be pronounced, make sure to practice saying it rather than cutting it down.

It is also possible to help the person you are talking to the favor of saving them from having to recall your personal name. Introduce yourself to the person, without waiting for them to inquire about your name, regardless of whether it's an acquaintance you've had a chance to meet previously. This will avoid from awkwardness if they've forgotten your name. It is possible to say, "Hi, Samuel, (say your name). What's up?" This will really alleviate tension and let people move on to having a relaxed conversation.

Infiltrate the conversation of others

If you are unable to locate the "approachable" person in the room , and everyone else is engaged in conversation with other people which makes you feel excluded What to do? make an effort to politely start a conversation. A good way to break the silence in a group the course of conversation is by waiting an intervalduring which the two people have remained silent for a few seconds or are just finishing discussing something specific. After the interval has ended then gently ask the individual who you don't want to discuss with for permission to speak to the other person you're interested in speaking to. After that, ask the other person's permission if you could speak with them later.

If you're working with a large group There are many ways to get the attention of your audience. Start by listening to the main speaker but be sure to sit in a position slightly away from the crowd. Allow them to be used to seeing your presence in the room and, if they're welcoming and open, they'll be more likely to let you in. Be aware of how they respond when you are present, for instance, whether they want your opinion or the way they look friendly.

It is essential to make sure that the group is warm with you. Therefore, make sure to identify positive aspects of the conversation, like the points of mutual agreement. Even though it could appear that you're too friendly however, you'll actually seem friendly and not threatening to the group unlike one who appears too assertive or, even more notably even arrogant.

Chapter 14: Presenting Body Language that is Approachable

When you're speaking to someone who is your first contact, it's essential to ensure they feel comfortable. If you don't it will be difficult for the conversation to be able to last or be a complete waste of time. The first step to start an informal conversation or having a conversation is to exhibit your body language to convey that "I'm friendly". When you are able to show an open posture and a relaxed posture, you can encourage people to engage with you since they'll feel like they are able to relax when they're with you. Here are some helpful tips on how to accomplish this:

Be sure to keep your phone out of sight. Doing a continuous check on your phone when you're in conversation with someone is among the most unprofessional things you could do. This is only acceptable in the case an emergency or when something unexpected happens to pop to light and requires immediate action, but when you're using it to check your Facebook then it is considered unprofessional. If you're looking to engage in conversation it is best to avoid looking frequently at your smartphone. You can put your phone on silence so that you will not receive a constant stream of messages. If someone truly needs help then they will make a phone call. The habit of checking on your mobile every couple of minutes isn't just unpleasing to the person you're communicating with, it's also inconsiderate.

Smile. A smile can create positive feelings. If you're someone who enjoys smiling people are more likely to engage with you. Smiles give people the impression that you're warm and welcoming. It's also easier to speak to those who are always smiling as you believe that they is enjoying talking to you. Smiles are also an indication of politeness and respect. It makes people feel like you're not bored of the conversation and you're really interested in what you are hearing from the other person.

Maintain proper eye contact. The eyes are extremely powerful. They convey information in a way words are unable to. When you're having a short talks or launching a conversation be sure you're in eye contact with your audience. Avoid looking towards the ground or the ceiling as this creates the impression that you don't have any clue what you're talking about. Some might think that this is a sign of being insincere. Both of you will be more comfortable by maintaining eye contact, however it shouldn't be excessive. Learn when and when to turn away and the best time and method to turn your attention back to the partner's eyes.

Keep your posture open. If you are making small-talk be sure to keep a straight posture. Avoid crossing either of your feet or folding the arms, as these movements could signal you're not ready for conversations. Instead, keep your legs and arms relaxed while using your hands to make appropriate gestures. Be flexible and do not slouch as this posture indicates disrespect and lack of interest. Be aware that when meeting somebody for the very first time you must let them know that you are friendly and willing to speak to them.

Maintain proper distance. If you don't know someone that well you do, don't remain too close to the person. A distance between you and the person you are talking to shows respect and respect. Don't be too close or away from the person you're talking to , as this could be a sign of a variety of things like unfriendliness or inappropriate motives.

If you are talking to someone in the beginning, ensure you remember these tips to ensure that you do not from sending negative and indirect messages to the person you are talking to. Be aware of these guidelines can help you progress your conversation and grow into a positive and engaging conversation.

Chapter 15: Display Your Personality

Everyone has qualities they are proud of, and also some that they would prefer not to possess. This is true to everyone, not just you. However, that shouldn't stop you from not having the time to enjoy socializing.

Whatever your personality is, you can become appealing and attractive. It is possible that you don't see yourself as a charismatic person but if you allow your personality to shine, you could become the most liked person.

Technique #19 Be Charismatic

Charisma is more than one trait in your personality. It's a mix of various traits that attract people to you.

Certain people are born with charisma. However, you can grow into an empathetic person. You can develop the ability to be charismatic by developing the traits and behavior which are common to charismatic individuals.

Do's and Don'ts

Being charismatic begins when you let the good aspects in your character shine. There are a few things to be aware of, however.

Do share your thoughts and opinions

To be a person of interest to be a dynamic person, you must not be afraid to share your opinions and thoughts. However, this does not mean you have to be a snob. You are able to express your thoughts without having to force others to agree with or take them into consideration.

The trick is to "respectfully be respectfully disagree" with the views of another. Be aware that if have the right to speak your opinions, others are also entitled to that right.

Learn to be able to compromise. The idea is further developed in a different chapter.

Don't be loud and obnoxious.

The world will have a person who is never loud and inconsiderate and, often, it causes misunderstandings and conflict.

Don't be the type of person. Be aware of the tone and that you speak at. Be alert and always be sure you behave in a manner that is appropriate.

Many people are not aware that they're acting loud and rude; it's probably not hurt to summon a family member or friend if they start to behave unintentionally.

Do not be afraid to share your interests and your Passion

Passionate people are never able to stop talking about things they love. They're always willing to talk about their interests and what they're passionate about. You can be that person.

Don't Get Bored!

What can you do to avoid becoming boring? Certain people, whether deliberately or not, take over conversations. They often speak without paying attention.

When you are at a moment of conversation and you are sharing something that you're passionate about, there's the tendency to continue talking, not considering the people around you.

Be aware of your actions. Allow the others to also speak. They may have a great story or an idea to talk about. Don't dominate any conversation as it would be rude and unprofessional.

Do practice empathy

It is important to be able to comprehend other people's situations and their feelings. Try to put yourself in the shoes of others. This will help you be able to better understand the person you are talking to. It also gives you an occasion to help the other person.

Empathy can help you let others feel like they are respected, not being ignored.

Beware of negative thoughts and behavior

One of the most effective methods of making people love your character is to show an optimistic attitude. People will avoid your persona if you're negative.

Being positive every day doesn't mean you don't recognize difficulties and obstacles.

Being optimistic is recognizing the opportunity to gain knowledge when problems arise. Being positive means choosing not to dwell on the issues but instead on the solutions that are possible.

It's not a quick process. It's a gradual process. If you're not charismatic, you must wait until you've changed your life, including embracing your positive characteristics, removing undesirable habits, and changing your perspective in your life.

Chapter 16: Utilizing Conversation to Make Deep Connections

It's essential for introverts to be honest, however it's not a bad idea to confirm that you have heard something that you like and be open to recognizing similarities since they're beneficial. If you have conversations with an individual about issues that are important you develop a greater knowledge of them and can open the door to all sorts of possibilities. If, for instance, someone you're discussing with comes up with ideas that are similar to your own and you agree, there's no reason not to express your agreement.

How can we take the conversation to higher levels of significance

The open-ended questions you ask give you the chance to listen further. People who listen actively have more to learn and are typically more than others. If you notice that you share common topics during the conversation, you may think of more ways to express your thoughts other than through words.

Let's look at an instance:

Ian is an introvert, and was having a conversation with an individual known as Katy. At one point , he asked her what she would imagine doing as young to which she replied, "Flying". When he learned of Katy's dream it brought him back to his youth when his dreams were like hers. He also learned of an indoor skydiving center that could inspire the childhood dream. Instead of discussing it, he decided that the best way to communicate their similarities was to go with her on a skydiving adventure. On the next day, after renting bikes, he took her to the location that matched the vision she had told him about. She was amazed and was able to see that the connection between them was stronger than she ever could have imagined. There was no point in conversation, but through being attentive, she was able to see that he was completely in her.

Naturally it's a particular example. It does illustrate how important it is to take the context of conversations and adding more details to enhance its meaning.

The most important topics to avoid when trying to create significant connections with other people are a few taboo subjects such as the news, weather, or the most recent dinner you've eaten. If you stay clear of the same questions and instead focus on broad, more engaging questions we've previously discussed and you'll achieve three main things:

you won't be enduring boring monotonous conversations

You will create a solid base for your relationship

and

You will discover if you are interested in developing a relationship with the person.

The ability to be authentic is essential for introverts. We are looking to be authentic about who we really are [KFW3However, small talk is a major deterrent and can make us feel unsatisfied. It's like getting ready for dinner and then having to jump through hoops until you are able to sit down and eat. The authenticity can be maintained with pre-planned questions that make way for conversation that is important not those that have without purpose or meaning. You would like to be closer to your friends however, they're familiar with conversations that are merely for fun. But the thing is that nobody can really build an intimacy with small conversations. They aren't aware of any other way to initiate conversations or get to know individuals, so they cling to the conventional. It's not necessary to be doing this, and I'm sure you wouldn't like doing this. I'm sure you'd rather be you and be a logical person. You now have the means to be yourself and it can give you an incredibly distinct advantage over your peers. If you have conversations planned that allow you to remain true to yourself and you can entice others to be the same and encourage them to build relationships between you.

Let's look at an instance of a woman known as Danielle:

Danielle was employed in an office. Every week, three of the most dreadful meetings were scheduled. They were of no use and were full of a lot of conversation. In order to be genuine efficient, she started to establish a reason in wanting to be there. Danielle began to tell her colleagues and her manager her fear of these meetings, and the reasons the reasons why she believed they were useless. Her manager thought that the small chat was just a way to bond however, she could recognize the shortcomings it brought to productivity. Through careful ideas and brainstorming in conjunction with the meetings coordinator they were able to make meetings more productive. The result was a four-point strategy consisting of just one meeting per week, for an hour, and having the purpose of each quarter within the hour. Everyone loved it as it added meaning to the meetings, and her supervisor realized that the new method of creating a plan for the meeting was more efficient. Danielle was able of being real and her honesty was admired by everyone who attended these gatherings.

If you are looking to be the person you are, be upfront about it right from the beginning. Consider alternatives to doing things that are compatible to your beliefs, yet serve other people. You'll retain your authentic self while improving the lives of everyone around you. There's no need to be a fake or pretend to conform to social rules. Introverts are renowned for their unique thinking process and preference for having moments of quiet. It's this ability, you'll discover it, that allows you to come up with innovative ideas. Simply by bringing clarity and purpose to your work place (or your social event) and not letting it be a place for useless gossip that has no effect will make you an instant celebrity.

Chapter 17: Avoid Unfortunate Silences

The long-awaited silent silence...

It's not only a problem during conversations. Silence refers to the absence of deliberate or deliberate sound. Intentional sounds are those that humans create, such as conversations as well as singing, but also things like music or the use of devices such as tapping the keyboard on laptops. The other sound that remains are not something that we can block. They're inevitable, and many find them disturbing.

A lot of people are not comfortable when there is silence or any type. Many of them have an physical reaction like hairs growing at the nape of their necks in a room that is silent especially in the dark. It is such a common situation that horror films use silicone in order to keep us and effectively.

Silence is a fear that is real.

Sedatephobia is a term used to describe this type of fear. It manifests as symptoms such as nausea sweating, panic attacks and breathlessness. The reason for this fear is usually an experience that was traumatic that the sufferer has experienced, like being imprisoned for a time.

Your aversion to silence might not be so extreme, but it is still uncomfortable. There is no one else like you. We've been taught to feel uncomfortable in silence. The mind is accustomed to the sound. The hum of traffic. The sound of a refrigerator. Background music at the grocery store as well as in elevators. The majority of us grew up in a home in which there was background music or some other kind of noise to cut out noise, like the TV running even though there was no one watching it.

The louder our world is thanks to the advancement of technologies and social media the more people are disturbed by the silence. Although the hum of our world creates a sense of discord with silence, it doesn't end there. Silence forces us to pay attention to our thoughts. These thoughts may cause anxiety, and noise is not able to distract us from.

It's true that the lack of sound isn't the only thing that can be frightening. It is more the absence of distraction from your thoughts. So, to overcome the fear of discomfort that comes with silence, it is essential to accept your thoughts and direct them in a manner that doesn't trigger anxiety. There are many ways to help yourself become more relaxed and at peace. This could practice mindfulness, and engage in a quiet pursuit like reading or meditation.

Although being comfortable in silence is great however, it's not something you would like to happen in the middle of a conversation. Learn more about the best ways to avoid it from happening.

How to Prevent Awkward Silences

Although silence isn't always a bad thing regardless of how many people in a conversation but awkward silence is the most definitive sign of a conversation regardless of whether it's a small conversation or something more substantial has not succeeded. Because we would like your conversation abilities to be as efficient as possible , this is the one scenario we'll try to avoid as often as we can.

Fortunately, there are strategies that you can employ to stay away from this type of occurrence. The first is to prepare the script for your talk in advance of time by using the CCAQ method. The brain is a muscle similar to any other muscle inside your body. The more you work it, the more powerful it gets.

The majority of the skill in small talk is due to the improvement of mental endurance and preparation. In other words, the more you do it, the more adept your brain will be in understanding the nuances of small talking. One of the best ways to get practiced before you speak to anyone is to write down an outline that your brain will be able to use regardless of whether you're nervous or shy, or just feeling out of your element. If you give your brain this option to go back to it will be less overwhelmed during conversations, and you are more apt to respond on the reaction of others when you talk.

Another method to ensure that conversations flow and that crickets don't disrupt the conversation you're making in small conversations is to make sure that your answers aren't monotonous. Be sure to avoid answering only "yes" or "no" to questions. They can be a distraction and will end small talk.

Instead, you can expand on these answers, and then come back with a new question to your personal.

For instance when you are asked a question that is not open-ended such as, "Are you enjoying the temperatures we're experiencing this day?" Instead of answering with a simple "yes" you could say, "Yes, I love the warm days that come with summer. What is your favourite season?" In this case you will notice that the conversation didn't follow a straight out. Actually, the conversation was the participants were encouraged to keep the conversation going in a positive way which provided participants with more details about each other.

Another method to make sure awkward silence does not encroach on conversations is to discuss details about yourself in small increments. When you slowly feed to the other person small bits of information about you and your life, conversations are allowed to grow. In contrast, if you verbally spit out everything you believe the other wants to know about the conversation will end in a matter of minutes, and of course you're still in silence and must be filled.

You should also know when it's time to alter the topic and how to change it well. Sometimes , small talk leads to an area that can cause discomfort. It is essential to read the crowd and guide the conversation away from the dangerous zone quickly.

There are several subtle shifts you can employ to direct the conversation in a way that permits this space between you and the person to be successful. This can include:

* "Going back to the things you've said earlier ..."

* "I am aware that this may appear to be out of the blue but ..."

* "This subject is totally unrelated however ..."

* "Oh wow! Take a look at.." and then point out something that isn't threatening to make a comment about.

Another way in order to prevent awkward silence, is to build upon earlier statements that one of you made.

Sometimes , no matter how hard we attempt to avoid that uncomfortable silence interferes with our conversations. If this is the case, you, don't be worried. It's happened to all at some point or another. Take the situation as it is, and then try to determine what led to it. It could be an untruthful statement made. It could be a blank response. Perhaps you've not been able to find an area of common interest to discuss.

After having completed this, you are able for a way to express your appreciation in a humorous or positive manner or go on with the conversation by asking an open-ended inquiry or positive note on the other person's surroundings.

In some instances small talk isn't working between participants. Be aware of when to leave with grace and dignity. Just say "Please please forgive me" and then leave. Don't think about this incident and don't think of it as an insignificant failure. It is a reality for every person. Take the lessons learned and continue onto your next thrilling social event.

Conclusion

There is no way to master the art of small-talk, but we hope that this Book will help you. One of the most crucial things to do is establish a goal for a specific time period. Let's take the form of... next week I'll be making small conversations to five other people. It requires confidence, patience and a little bit of cheek however, you will eventually overcome your shyness.

It all starts with knowing what you should say and you should not say! If you are able to find the right balance between these two things, you're good to go. If you don't then don't fret. The purpose of the game is to win a few and then lose some.

You are able to determine the moment when the enthusiasm level of the other person drops to less than 50 percent. It's time to end the conversation to a halt.

Maybe , at a later time, with a different person.

These rules of conversation aren't set in stone. You are able to use your personal discretion to judge when you're progressing and when you're not. Keep in mind that each relationship, be it social, business or love one, starts with small talk in one way or another.

www.ingramcontent.com/pod-product-compliance
Lightning Source LLC
Chambersburg PA
CBHW071842080526
44589CB00012B/1087